Art and
Civilization

Other titles in the series
Art and Civilization:

Prehistory
Ancient Egypt
Ancient Rome
Ancient Greece
The Renaissance

Medieval Times

Giovanni Di Pasquale, Matilde Bardi

Illustrations by Studio Stalio (Alessandro Cantucci,
Fabiano Fabbrucci, Andrea Morandi, Ivan Stalio),
Manuela Cappon, Lorenzo Cecchi,
Luisa Della Porta, Andrea Ricciardi di Gaudesi

PETER BEDRICK BOOKS

McGraw-Hill
Children's Publishing
A Division of The **McGraw·Hill** Companies

This edition published in the United States in 2002 by
Peter Bedrick Books, an imprint of
McGraw-Hill Children's Publishing,
A Division of The McGraw-Hill Companies
8787 Orion Place
Columbus, OH 43240

www.MHkids.com

ISBN 0-87226-686-9

Library of Congress Cataloging-in-Publication Data is on file with the publisher

Medieval Times was created and produced by
McRae Books Srl, via de' Rustici, 5 – Florence (Italy)
e-mail: mcrae@tin.it

Text: Giovanni Di Pasquale, Matilde Bardi
Main Illustrations: Studio Stalio (Alessandro Cantucci,
Fabiano Fabbrucci, Andrea Morandi, Ivan Stalio), Manuela Cappon, Lorenzo Cecchi,
Luisa Della Porta, Andrea Ricciardi di Gaudesi
Picture research: Elzbieta Gontarska
Graphic design: Marco Nardi
Editing: Anne McRae, Loredana Agosta
Layout and cutouts: Laura Ottina, Adriano Nardi
Color separations: Fotolito Toscana, Florence and Litocolor, Florence

Printed in Italy

02 03 04 05 06 MCR 10 9 8 7 6 5 4 3 2 1

Contents

‡ *The alcazar (from the Arabic for "fortress") of Segovia, in Spain, was built in the 11th century and was used throughout the Middle Ages. It was badly damaged by a fire in 1862 and then rebuilt.*

Introduction

The period normally referred to as the Middle Ages comprises the thousand years between the fall of the Western Roman Empire (476 A.D.) and Christopher Columbus's discovery of America (1492). Though long considered as dark and unchanging ages, we now divide the medieval era into two distinct periods. Before the year 1000 we speak of the early Middle Ages, stretching from the end of the Roman world to the gradual emergence of Europe. The second period, known as the late Middle Ages and encompassing the 11th to 15th centuries, was a time of growth and transition that led to the Renaissance and the subsequent modern world. The early Middle Ages were mainly poor, primitive, underdeveloped, and rural. The later period was increasingly dynamic, with growing cities and towns, more trade and commerce, and advances in government and technology.

Castles

After the year 1000 A.D., Europe was divided into a network of small states, nominally under the authority of an emperor or king, but really independent. Their chief strength lay in the castle (from the diminutive of the Latin *castrum* used by the Romans to designate a military encampment). The castle's main purpose was to provide military defense, but it was also the residence of the local lords, and a center for their private and financial interests, as well as their political ambitions.

The Crusades

For almost 200 years, in the 11th to 13th centuries, the Christian popes, kings, and knights of Europe sent armies to fight the Muslims, who controlled Jerusalem and other important sites in the Holy Land. The first of eight Crusades was successful in 1099 in winning Jerusalem back from the "infidels," but the city was returned to Muslim rule under Saladin in 1187. The last crusaders were driven from the Holy Land by the Mameluke rulers in 1291.

A wealth of symbols

In the Middle Ages it was believed that every aspect of life concealed some hidden meaning, of which it was the "symbol." The Wheel of Fortune (left) was a frequent image and symbolized the belief that even kings could not escape the uncertainty of human destiny, since fate could cause anyone to be plunged into misfortune from one day to the next.

The cathedral of Notre Dame in Paris, France. With its huge, heavily sculpted doors and flying buttresses, it is a perfect example of the Gothic style of architecture.

Flying buttresses

The Gothic style

Gothic architecture first appeared in France during the 12th century. It was based on the use of large pillars that supported intersecting arches carrying vaults, while flying buttresses on the exterior offset their weight. This made it possible to build lofty cathedrals that were slender and well-proportioned despite their vast scale, soaring to great heights without appearing massive. Large stained-glass windows were set into the walls to illuminate and enhance the enormous interior spaces.

Huge, sculpted doors

The rebirth of the cities

After centuries of neglect, during the 10th century the cities and towns of Europe were reborn and gradually became the centers of a new social order. Many soon adopted self-government (the "communes" of Italy) and became the focal point of trade and commerce, as well as seats of learning.

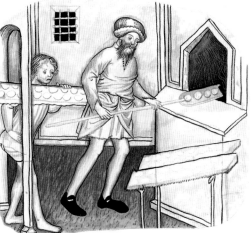

Among many occupations in the city, one of the most common was that of baker. The bread that all families made at home was taken by the women to be baked in the baker's oven.

The plague

In 1347, the plague that was thought to have been eradicated in the 8th century suddenly re-emerged in Europe. In four years, the epidemic swept over almost the whole continent, depleting the total population by almost a third. It brought an abrupt end to the increase in population that had occurred during the four preceding centuries.

Maestà, by Simone Martini (1315)

This fresco was commissioned by the government of Siena, Italy, and depicts the Enthroned Virgin and Child (1) beneath a baldachin (2), surrounded by angels and saints. The work served a strong civic purpose: the moral and religious principles of good government are written on the plinth (3) beneath the throne, while the Madonna symbolizes the city's communal spirit. In the foreground, there are two kneeling angels who offer lilies and roses in golden bowls to the Virgin (4) and the city's four patron saints Crescentian (5), Victor (6), Savinian (7), and Ansanus (8). St. John the Baptist (9), St. Peter (10), St. Catherine of Siena (11), and the archangels Gabriel (12) and Michael (13) are also depicted.

The Germanic Invasions

During the 5th century, following the economic and cultural decline of the Western Roman Empire, the stronger and better organized of the Germanic tribes, who had long been threatening the frontiers, conquered the Western provinces and established the so-called "Barbarian" kingdoms. The Franks settled in Northern Gaul, causing it to be known as France; the Visigoths settled in the area straddling the Pyrenees (between modern France and Spain); the Vandals occupied the African coast; and the Angles and Saxons moved to Ancient Britain. Odoacer, leader of the Heruli, deposed the last Western Roman emperor and ruled Italy from Ravenna, with the accord of the Eastern Roman emperor. He was driven out by the Ostrogoths led by King Theodoric, who attempted to unite his Germanic and Latin subjects. In 568 A.D., Italy suffered its final invasion at the hands of the Lombards.

This 4th century statue shows the two Roman emperors in an embrace to indicate harmony.

The decline of the Roman Empire

The Roman Empire became progressively weaker from the 3rd century onward. In 286, Emperor Diocletian split power in the Roman Empire under a system of government that included two emperors; one for the Eastern Empire and one for the Western Empire. Less than 50 years later, the emperor Constantine moved the capital from Rome to Constantinople, in the East. The poorer, less populated Western Empire was unable to withstand the invasions of the Germanic peoples form the North and East.

Visigoth votive crown in gold and precious stones. The pendants are shaped like letters of the alphabet and form the name of the king who commissioned it: Recesvind (653–672). The region of Andalusia ("Vandalusia") took its name from the Visigoths.

Many of the Germanic invaders, like the Saxon warrior shown here, fought on horseback using bows and arrows, shields, sabers, and lances.

Weapons

The arms of the Germanic, or Teutonic, warriors were different from those used by the Romans. One of the most common was the sax, a one-edged saber of varying size with a wooden or bone hilt that was sometimes so long that both hands were needed to wield it. It was used for fighting on horseback and also, in times of peace, for slaughtering animals.

Invaders and settlers

Germanic peoples had been trickling into the Western Empire for many years. At first, they were tolerated and absorbed into Roman society. Many joined the army and helped to defend the frontiers of the failing empire. But by the 5th century, the trickle had become a tidal wave and, when the Romans tried to stop them, they were overrun.

Below: Detail of a mosaic showing the palace of the Ostrogoth king, Theodoric the Great (c. 454–526), at Ravenna, capital of his kingdom in Italy.

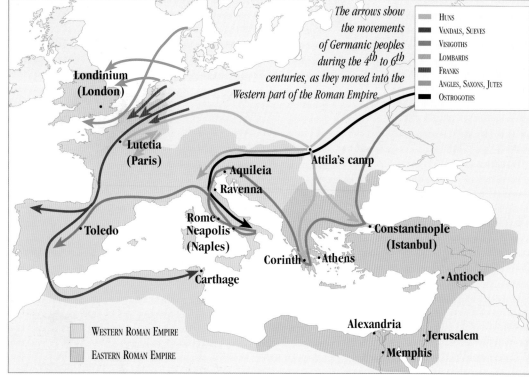

The arrows show the movements of Germanic peoples during the 4th to 6th centuries, as they moved into the Western part of the Roman Empire.

	HUNS
	VANDALS, SUEVES
	VISIGOTHS
	LOMBARDS
	FRANKS
	ANGLES, SAXONS, JUTES
	OSTROGOTHS

Londinium (London)

Lutetia (Paris)

Aquileia

Ravenna

Attila's camp

Rome
Neapolis (Naples)

Toledo

Corinth · Athens

Constantinople (Istanbul)

Carthage

Antioch

Alexandria

Jerusalem

Memphis

WESTERN ROMAN EMPIRE

EASTERN ROMAN EMPIRE

Germanic Invasions of the Roman Empire between the 4th and 6th centuries.

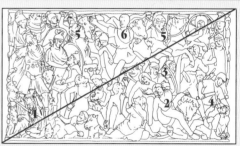

Gold Lombard fibula, 7th century. These clasps were used to secure garments and were worn by both men and women.

The last Germanic invasions

The European Middle Ages sprang from the clash of the Latin peoples with their northern neighbors. The Lombards (or Longobards) were the last intruders to install themselves in the former Roman territories, and between the 6th and 8th centuries, they occupied a large part of the Italian peninsula. The fusion that took place between the Roman and Germanic cultures formed the basis for many of the social, artistic, and legal aspects of medieval society.

A new society

The invasions led to massacres and famines that severely depopulated the countryside. The conquered lands were left partly to their original owners and partly divided among the soldiers, who became farmers and small landowners. The problem then arose of how the Romans and "Barbarians" could live peacefully together. This was gradually resolved by the merging of the two cultures.

This gold and copper plate decorated the helmet of the Lombard king, Agilulf (reigned 590–615). The king, seated on his throne in the center, is flanked by two warriors. Winged Victory figures celebrate his triumph, while two pairs of dignitaries bring him the crown. The influence of Roman art is obvious, showing the mingling of the two cultures.

The Ludovisi Sarcophagus

The Romans had clashed with Germanic tribes many times over the centuries. This relief carving from a 3rd-century sarcophagus shows a battle between the Romans and the Goths that took place in 251 A.D. at Abritto, in modern-day Bulgaria. The carving was made in honor of Erennius Etruscus and his father Decius, both of whom were killed in the battle.

The scene is divided in half by an imaginary line (1) running from bottom left to top right. The defeated Goths have been driven into the triangle on the bottom right, where they writhe in terror and suffering (2). Roman soldiers gather prisoners (3) or finish them off (4). Two victorious Roman horsemen ride through the center (5), while the young hero, Erennius (6), stands bareheaded, gazing off into the distance.

The Church

During the centuries of upheaval that followed the fall of the Roman Empire, the Church acquired great moral prestige and, in just a few hundred years, enormous political power. Strong popes like Gregory VII (1073–1085) and Innocent III (1198–1216) clashed with secular leaders to defend the supremacy of the Church which, in turn, continued to own and govern extensive and valuable territories. Many voices were raised calling on the Church to return to the poverty preached by the Gospels, as practiced by, for example, St. Benedict, who founded the Benedictine Order in 529 in Montecassino, in central Italy.

The Benedictine monastery of Cluny in France was founded in the year 909. In the 11th century the abbot of Cluny was the leader of a confraternity of over two hundred abbeys spread all over Europe and directly dependent on the pope.

Monasticism

St. Benedict (left) founded several monasteries, for which he composed a set of rules that were adopted over most of Europe. The monks, under the guidance of an abbot, were to live lives of prayer, and were to be devoted also to working in the scriptorium where texts were copied and translated. The monastic movement in Ireland was also important, and in the 7th century it spread the Gospel to islands in the Atlantic and to Germany. During the 12th century, the Cistercian Order was founded by St. Bernard of Clairvaux. Its monks were farmers and skilled craftsmen.

Monastic communities were often established in little-populated, marshy areas and the monks labored to make the barren land bear crops. With the aid of legacies and donations, many monasteries became big landowners over the years, employing large numbers of peasants. 12th-century illumination: a Cistercian monk and a peasant felling a tree to clear new farming land.

The Baptistry of the Arians (Ravenna, Italy)

This 5th-century mosaic is inside the dome of the Baptistry of the Arians. It shows Christ (1) being baptized by John the Baptist (2). This took place in the Jordan River, in this picture the river is shown as a person (3). The dove of the Holy Spirit (4) is shown above Christ's head. Twelve saints (5) are standing in the circle around the central scene. At the top, the empty throne (6) is a symbol in Byzantine Christian art of God, or of the Second Coming of Christ.

The first Basilica of St. Peter's, in Rome

In about 330 A.D., after the edict on tolerance that gave freedom of worship to Christians, building work began on a grand basilica dedicated to St. Peter, close to the site of his martyrdom. It had a rectangular plan and was divided into five naves by four rows of columns. A porticoed building was added in front to hold those waiting to be baptized. In the rear was a semicircular apse where the religious rites took place. This kind of church was to have a strong influence on all that were built later.

The Schism with the East

In the Byzantine world, Christianity assumed various new features that were not pleasing to the Roman Curia. In 1054, the disagreements between Rome and Constantinople caused the Great Schism, the separation of the two Churches, that led to the foundation of the Greek Orthodox

Pilgrimages

Pilgrimages were common events in the Middle Ages. People from all walks of life undertook these long and often dangerous journeys to reach venerated sites: the Holy Land, where Jesus had lived and preached; Rome, the city of martyrs; Santiago di Compostela in Spain, where the body of St. James was thought to have been miraculously washed ashore. Inns and hostels sprang up along the pilgrim trails. Anyone who threatened or robbed a pilgrim faced excommunication.

Left: This illustration comes from a 12ᵗʰ-century French guide for pilgrims heading for remote Compostela. It gives advice on things like the quality of the water along the route. It attacks greedy ferrymen and others who made unfair profits from the pilgrims.

This chalice (wine cup) was used in the Greek Orthodox Church.

The papacy

Roman Catholics believe that the pope is the heir to St. Peter and the Vicar of Christ on Earth. He is also the leading ecclesiastical authority. During the Middle Ages, the temporal, (earthly, political, and economic) power of the pope increased greatly and vied with the power of the emperor. This led to a series of struggles with varying outcomes, but the Church was the main winner.

Statue of Boniface VIII, the pope who proclaimed the first great Jubilee of 1300 in Rome.

This detail from a fresco by Giotto at Assisi, in Italy, shows St. Francis expelling devils from a medieval Tuscan city.

The devil

In medieval times, Christians believed they had a ferocious enemy who sought by any means possible to steal man's most precious possession, his soul. This terrible persecutor was the devil, a fallen angel and the greatest evil power, represented by the collective imagination in a variety of horrific forms and guises.

Nuns and convents

Women who wanted to devote their lives to Christianity were known as nuns, and they lived in convents or nunneries that were usually separate from monasteries. Not all women entered convents for religious reasons. Some were sent for refusing to obey their fathers or husbands, while others went because they had lost their homes.

This fresco, by Giotto, shows St. Francis giving his cloak to a poor man.

St. Francis and St. Domenic

Early in the 13ᵗʰ century, Francis, a wealthy young man of Assisi, publicly renounced his family inheritance and committed himself to the observance of absolute poverty, in accordance with the Gospel. However, his followers did not cut themselves off from the world, but preached in towns and cities and supported themselves by begging. In the 13ᵗʰ century another successful order was founded by St. Domenic. It set out to combat heresies (doctrines that were at odds with the teachings of the Church).

The Byzantine Empire

While invasions raged in the West, the Eastern, or Byzantine Empire stood firm. Its borders were easier to defend, its population larger, and its economy more dynamic. The Byzantine fleet was always to keep the trading routes with the West open. Byzantine civilization was based on the structure of Roman government, Greek language and culture, and the Christian religion. Furthermore, Byzantium was a bridge between East and West, open to many and various influences. The Byzantines were proud of being a Christian Empire and took their role as defenders of the faith against pagans and heretics very seriously.

Emperor Constantine (reigned 305–337 A.D.), moved the capital of the Empire from Rome to Constantinople, a city he founded on the site of the ancient city of Byzantium, in modern Turkey. Constantinople was to become known as the "New Rome."

This image (below) shows co-emperors Michael I and Leo V in 813.

The walls of Byzantium

The massive walls of Byzantium were built in 413 when the city was still called Constantinople. The walls covered four miles and had 192 watchtowers, visible proof of the city's strength and unassailability. During the 5th century, they protected the city from the "Barbarians" sweeping down from the Eastern European steppes and, in the 7th and 8th centuries, from Arab attacks. But in 1204, they failed to halt the Crusaders and the Venetians, who captured the city. Its final fall was in 1453, at the hands of the Turks.

The Byzantine emperor

The emperor of Byzantium was the object of a quasi-religious cult in which traditionally Roman elements became blended with Eastern ones. In his presence all subjects, even leading dignitaries, were obliged to prostrate themselves on the ground. He was considered to be God's representative on Earth, which is why he was always shown with a halo.

Women and power

Many Byzantine empresses enjoyed great power, sometimes openly and sometimes more covertly. Theodora, the wife of Justinian, was forceful and active in political life. She held considerable influence over her husband.

A carved ivory panel shows Empress Irene (c. 752–803) who first ruled jointly with her son, Constantine VI, but then had him imprisoned and ruled alone.

Byzantine wealth

Merchants in Byzantine towns imported silks and spices from China, and timber and furs from Western and Northern Europe. Silkworms were introduced into the empire in the 6th century, when the manufacture of silk textiles became important. These were later exported, along with carved ivory, enamel, and glassware. Trade prospered under powerful emperors such as Basil II (c. 958–1025), who was known as Bulgaroctonus, or "Slayer of the Bulgars."

The wealth of the Byzantines came as a shock to the European knights of the Fourth Crusade, who captured Constantinople in 1204. The crusaders sacked the city and stole as much of its riches as they could. These horses (left) were brought back to the Italian city of Venice, where they can still be seen today. The episode highlighted the rift between the Western and Eastern Christians.

The face of Christ, disfigured by iconoclasts, in an image carried to Calabria, in Italy, by monks fleeing from persecution.

Iconoclasm

Early in the 8th century, a movement began to spread across the Byzantine Empire that condemned the opulence and wealth of the Church, which was thought to be at odds with the simplicity of the early faith. The result was the destruction of holy images (known as iconoclasm). It was also influenced by Islam and Judaism which forbade the representation of God. In 717, the Emperor Leo III ordered all icons to be destroyed and Church property confiscated, but this initiative faded over the course of a few decades.

The monks in the mountains

From the 10th century on, self-supporting hermitages and monasteries were built in the most isolated areas of Mount Athos (Sacred Mount), in Northern Greece. In the 12th century, Mount Athos was the home not only of Greek religious men but also of Russians, Armenians, Italians, and Georgians. Today, it is a monastic republic under the political rule of Greece. It is not easy to visit and entrance is strictly forbidden to women.

Mosaic of Justinian and his Retinue (mid-6th century, San Vitale, Ravenna, Italy)
Justinian (reigned 527–565 A.D.) was one of the greatest Byzantine emperors. Here, he is shown wearing royal purple robes and crowned with a halo (1). Justinian played an important role in Byzantine history in many areas, including war, religion, culture, and administration. He was responsible for the monumental task of revising and amending Roman law, the *corpus iuris civilis*. He also attempted, without success, to reunite the original Roman Empire. He is flanked by Maximian, Bishop of Ravenna (2), imperial dignitaries (3), guards (4), and prelates (5).

Islam

Arabia was a mixed region of fertile areas with plenty of water where there were cities engaged in trading, and the desert, inhabited by Bedouins, a nomadic people who raised animals, traded on caravan routes, and carried out raids. Following the preaching of Mohammed, the whole region became unified and a series of conquests began that led to the creation of an enormous and powerful empire, where the arts, culture, sciences, and commerce all flourished.

Right: A silver hand symbolizing the Five Pillars of Islam and the protective hand of Fatima, Mohammed's daughter.

The astrolabe was used to determine the position of the sun and other stars in the sky. Sailors used it to establish their routes.

Left: The archangel Gabriel appears to Mohammed and begins to reveal Allah's message to him.

The sciences

The Arabs were highly advanced in the sciences. They took a keen interest in geography, mathematics, and astronomy, and introduced the numerals of the decimal system (still known as "Arabic") and the concept of zero, though all were originally drawn from India. They were skilled in irrigation techniques and introduced paper into Europe to replace parchment.

The Koran

The Sacred Book (al-Qur'an, the Koran), which Mohammed declared to have been in part dictated directly by the archangel Gabriel, has 114 chapters, called *suras*, arranged in order of diminishing length and identified by headings. Each *sura* is composed of separate verses. The Koran is the fundamental source of Islam, a word which means "to surrender (to God)." A true believer is called a Muslim.

Mohammed

Mohammed was born in Mecca in about 570 A.D. As a young man, he worked as a camel trader, traveling around the Arabian peninsula and coming into contact with both Judaism and Christianity. His marriage to a rich widow, Khadija, at the age of 24, relieved him of material worries and allowed him to devote himself to religious contemplation. He began to preach in around 610, but in 622 he was obliged to flee to Medina to escape persecution. This flight (know as "the Hegira") marks the beginning of the Muslim calendar. In 630, the prophet returned to Mecca with an army, but died shortly afterward in Medina (632).

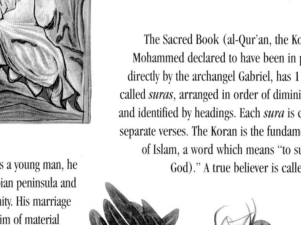

A Caravan of merchants from a 13th-century Arabian miniature.

The Five Pillars of Islam

Mohammed preached a faith that was "revealed" and monotheistic, like Judaism and Christianity. It was founded on the Five Pillars of Islam: belief in one God, the omnipotent creator; daily prayer; ritual fasting during the ninth month (Ramadan) of the Islamic lunar year; at least one pilgrimage to Mecca in a lifetime; and almsgiving as set out in the law.

Luxuries by camel

The interior of the Arabian peninsula was inhabited by Bedouin tribes, who lived as nomadic herdsmen. Agriculture was restricted to the oases. However, along the coast of the Red Sea, there were busy communities of traders who carried luxury goods from the East (spices, perfumes, highly-prized wood, precious stones, and incense) toward the Mediterranean from where the Byzantines distributed them to the West.

Left: An Arabic bazaar is a covered market where all kinds of goods are sold. This early 13th-century illustration shows a jeweler, a pharmacist, a butcher, and a baker.

Muslim Astronomers at Work

This scene comes from an Ottoman manuscript and shows Muslim astronomers at work in a 16th-century observatory in Istanbul. Even though it depicts a time at the very end of the Middle Ages (1575), all of the instruments shown were used by medieval Muslim scientists. On the far side of the table, two astronomers examine an astrolabe (1). On their right, a man is looking through an alidad attached to a quadrant (2). On the far left, another astronomer looks through a diopter (3). The table (4) is littered with more instruments, while scientists in the foreground study a globe (5) and take notes and discuss a manuscript (6).

The miniature below shows a lance-bearing Christian force struggling against Muslim warriors during the Second Crusade, in 1147–48.

The Crusades

The First Crusade was proclaimed in 1096. Its aim was to free the holy Christian sites from Muslim domination. Many European knights set off eastward and, in 1099, they conquered Jerusalem. Over the course of time, various Christian realms were founded (Kingdom of Jerusalem, Principality of Antioch, Country Palatine of Edessa) but they only survived until the 13th century. The last Crusade ended in failure in 1270.

The Extent of the Islamic World about 800.

ITALY

BLACK SEA
• Constantinople

Cordoba
Seville • Granada

MEDITERRANEAN SEA

SYRIA
Damascus • Baghdad
Alexandria
Jerusalem

Cairo

RED SEA
• Medina
• Mecca

INDIAN OCEAN

Arab expansion

The great period of Islamic expansion began in the mid-7th century. First, Syria, Egypt, and Palestine were seized from the Byzantine Empire, and then North Africa and the Persian Empire were conquered. Baghdad replaced Mecca as the Islamic capital. Later expansion involved Central Asia, India, and Spain. In the 9th century, the Arabs took Sicily and controlled the Mediterranean. The reasons for this expansion lie in the religious fervor that sustained the Holy War (jihad), the Muslims' tolerance of the conquered peoples, and the internal weakness of the other leading powers of the time (the Byzantine and Persian empires).

Saladin (1137–1193) was one of the greatest Muslim leaders to oppose the marauding Christian knights. He led the force that recaptured Jerusalem from the crusaders in 1187, ending an 88-year occupation by Christians.

The Feudal Age

During the 9th and 10th centuries, Europe was invaded once more, this time by peoples from the icy North and Western Asia. After the invasions, most of Europe was ruled by kings, each of whom reigned over an independent realm. They introduced a form of social organization that historians now refer to as "feudalism." Under this system, a king divided his land among the most powerful nobles who, in return, offered military service and allegiance to his realm. The great nobles then granted land to lesser nobles and knights in return for the same kind of loyalty, and so on down through the social hierarchy. The serfs, or peasants, were on the bottom of the social scale and they received land from local lords in exchange for produce and work. Feudalism weakened after the plague struck in the 14th century, when the great drop in population gave the lower classes greater bargaining power.

In the 10th century some groups of Norsemen settled in Normandy in northwestern France where they established a stable duchy, their base for the conquest of England and Southern Italy. The illustration below, a detail from the Bayeaux Tapestry, shows the Normans attacking England in 1066.

Right: Crown of Stephen I, king of Hungary. The Magyars, who invaded Europe in the 9th century, settled in Hungary. Stephen was crowned first king of Hungary on Christmas Day, 1000.

Left: a Viking warrior's heavy metal helmet.

Below: Saracens attacking Sicily, in Italy, in the 9th century.

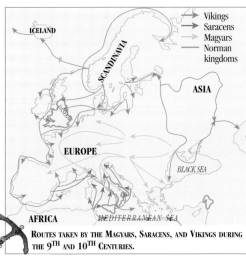

ROUTES TAKEN BY THE MAGYARS, SARACENS, AND VIKINGS DURING THE 9TH AND 10TH CENTURIES.

The invasions of the 9th and 10th centuries

From the end of the 8th century onward, Europe was invaded from three different directions. The Norsemen ("men of the North," or Vikings, as they were called) were a Scandinavian people who spread out in various directions during the 8th century because their communities were overpopulated. They reached Russia, Iceland, Ireland, and England. They sacked cities and major towns, like Bordeaux and Lisbon, and by sailing upriver even raided the rural areas. At about the same time, Arab Saracens attacked from the south, spreading the Islamic faith across Southern Europe. A third set of invaders, the Magyars, raided Central Europe from their homelands in Eastern Europe.

The Holy Roman Empire

When the Carolingian dynasty died out, it was replaced by other dynasties, usually of German origin, that ruled over what became known in the 13th century as the Holy Roman Empire. Charlemagne's empire was first reunited in 962 by Otto the Great. It continued under different families and with varying degrees of power and land until 1806, when Francis II of the house of Habsburg-Lorraine resigned the title of Holy Roman Emperor. During the Middle Ages, the Holy Roman Empire usually covered the modern lands of Germany, Austria, the Czech Republic, Switzerland, Eastern France, Holland, and Northern Italy.

Below: Charles the Great, or Charlemagne, was the most powerful of the Carolingian rulers and one of the greatest kings of the Middle Ages. He was crowned in Rome on December 25, 800, by Pope Leo III.

The Carolingians

The Carolingian dynasty replaced the earlier Merovingian ruling family in France in the mid-8th century. The Carolingians were at their greatest under Charlemagne, who not only vastly increased the area over which the family ruled, but also introduced enlightened forms of governing and bureaucracy which encouraged economic and social progress throughout Europe. On his death his empire was split among his heirs who were all much weaker rulers.

Right: Frederick I, also known as Barbarossa or "Red Beard," was a popular king of the Hohenstaufen dynasty, who became Holy Roman Emperor in 1155. He died in the Holy Land during the Crusades.

Courtly Love; Ladies watch Knights Jousting

During the 11th century, a new ideal for courtly love appeared in medieval literature. According to this concept, knights wooed and worshiped married ladies, serving them in relationships that were very similar to those that existed between the vassals and lords. This scene, carved in ivory on the back of a medieval mirror, shows knights (1) and (2) jousting before a "Castle of Love" (3). Ladies (4) stand on the ramparts (5) watching the men fight. At the very top, Cupid (6) shoots an arrow toward one of the women, who appears to be swooning with love.

Left: This illumination shows the pope and the emperor seated on one throne in a brotherly embrace. In reality, the pope and the Holy Roman Emperor were almost always at loggerheads.

Above: Relief sculpture showing Otto II investing, or appointing, a bishop.

Two suns under a single sky

Initially, the popes in Rome supported the Holy Roman Emperor. But as time went by they became bitter enemies, fighting over many different issues and dividing Europe into two camps. The so-called Investiture Dispute, about whether the pope was the only one who could appoint bishops, was particularly long and bitter. Of course, all the disputes could be brought back to the same point – who was the more powerful of the two rulers.

Right: Detail from a medieval miniature showing Roland during the Battle of Roncesvalles, fought in 778.

Les chansons de geste ("Songs of deeds")

More than 80 epic poems, or "songs," celebrating the life and times of Charlemagne and his heirs have survived. The earliest and most well-known of these is called *La Chanson de Roland* ("The Song of Roland"). It celebrates a battle that took place in the Pyrenees Mountains between Charlemagne's troops and the Saracens.

War

The Middle Ages were marked by long and repeated wars that led, over the course of the centuries, to a complete transformation in the techniques of fighting, weapons, fortification, and methods of defense. Military supremacy was vital, as was the reputation of a king when a city's survival could depend on a single battle. In 10th-century Europe, military life chiefly concerned the nobles, whose strength lay in their castles, but from the 11th century onward, the cities also had defensive walls and towers.

Coats of arms, also called shields of arms, date back to the Middle Ages when they were worn by knights in battle to establish their identity. A heavily armored knight was unrecognizable; the coat of arms served to show enemies and friends who he was. Later, they came to show family membership, alliances, ownership of property, and profession.

Left: In this illustration from the great epic poem, the Song of Roland, Charlemagne's army is being attacked in the Pyrenees Mountains, while returning to France after a failed campaign to reconquer Spain from the Muslims.

The castle: fortress and dwelling place

Many different kinds of castles were built, and they had numerous functions. They were all intended as military strongholds, but they also served as places where the people who lived scattered over the countryside could meet and where noble families could be suitably housed. Inside the walls, there was usually a main tower; a church or chapel; a large hall where justice was administered and knights gathered; and working areas such as cellars, storerooms, wells, stables, and hay barns.

Guidoriccio da Fogliano, by Simone Martini (1330)

This fresco shows two medieval castles – Montemassi (1) and Sassoforte (2) – in Central Italy, that came under the rule of Siena when they were taken by troops led by Guidoriccio da Fogliano, the knight shown here advancing with all the confidence of a victor (3). The fresco shows the castles, knight, and the besiegers' encampment (4) in a very realistic way. The tents (5), stockades (6), lances (7), and banners (8) are all clearly visible.

Knights in shining armor

During the 13th century a knight's armor consisted of a hauberk, or chain mail garment, protecting the throat and chest that was worn over a leather tunic, and a chain mail hood worn under a helmet. Other, smaller pieces of armor, such as mail hose and steel shin guards, protected the legs. Over the top, knights wore cloth overgarments bearing their family's coat of arms. War horses had some padded protection and displayed the knight's heraldry, or coats of arms.

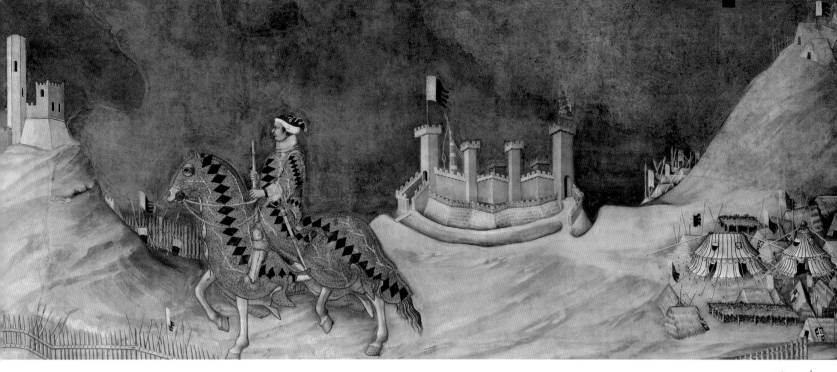

The crossbow

The crossbow was developed from the longbow and allowed greater precision, although it had a shorter range. There were light crossbows, used by foot-soldiers and knights, and heavy standing crossbows, used during sieges on towns and castles. In the 13th century it was adopted all over Europe, with the result that knights' breastplates had to be reinforced to withstand heavier blows.

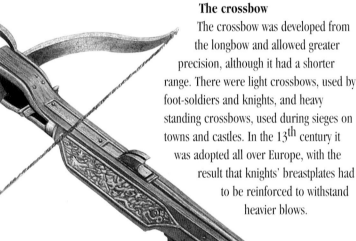

This 14th-century French illustration shows knights cutting into the base of a castle's walls while its defenders tried to smash their protective wooden covering from above.

War machines

The trebuchet (above), stood up to 50 feet tall (15 meters), and had a long arm activated by a series of counterweights. It was used to hurl heavy rocks at the enemy. Other war machines included the battering-ram, a heavy beam mounted on wheels used to break down walls or gates; and the catapult, a wooden bar drawn back under great pressure that sprang forward when released, hurling missiles at the walls.

Greek fire, a terrible secret weapon

In naval battles, Byzantine forces used what was known as Greek fire, an incendiary substance that was spread with a siphon and was not extinguishable by water. The formula was a closely guarded secret.

Besieged and besiegers

A castle's walls were always topped by a walkway protected by battlements from which the besieged could pour boiling water or oil, and hurl stones down on the attackers. This was the only method of withstanding a siege. The besiegers dug tunnels below the walls where they lit fires to burn them down.

The City

After the collapse of the Roman world, the face of ancient cities gradually began to change. The drop in the number of inhabitants caused some areas inside the walls to become abandoned or to be turned into farmland. Many of the Roman city features, such as drains, aqueducts, and roads, were no longer cared for and were damaged or fell into disuse. When the economy improved after the 11th century, the cities began to develop again, and new stone buildings, city walls, and squares were built.

In many cities of Roman origin, the ancient monuments were incorporated into later buildings. In a piazza in Lucca, Italy, for example (below), private houses were built in the amphitheater. We can still see the oval shape of the Roman Building.

The town hall

By the end of the 12th century, many city governments had their seat in a town hall (here we see the one in Siena, Italy), that usually stood in the main square. This is where the citizens' general assemblies were held, justice was administered, and funds of public money were stored. Very often these buildings resembled fortresses with thick walls and towers, but they were also decorated with frescoes and sculptures to display a city's importance and wealth.

Some houses had a primitive outside lavatory. This illustration (below) comes from a 15th-century edition of the Decameron *by Giovanni Boccaccio (1313–75), a collection of stories told by young people who fled the plague-ridden streets of Florence in 1348.*

Garbage

The absence of drains and sewers was one of the chief problems in a medieval city. Even organic waste was thrown out of the window, and there was a constant risk of epidemics.

Medieval towns were very busy, with people coming and going to visit shops and especially the market. People from outside the town brought their wares to sell, and the narrow streets were full of pedlars. Town gates were opened at dawn and closed at dusk. Merchants often had to pay a toll to enter.

Green areas

Inside the city walls, there were large unbuilt areas where fruit trees, medicinal herbs, and vegetables were grown. The wealthier families often turned them into the gardens we find described in literature of the period, delightful places where music was played and romantic meetings took place.

The walls

Almost all medieval cities were surrounded by walls. Many were rebuilt and enlarged during the 10th century to hold the new buildings that were erected during the economic recovery that took place after 1000. They were entered through large gates, often named after saints, with manned guardhouses. The encircling walls were set with towers that were normally spaced a bow-shot away from each other, enabling the whole length of the fortification to be defended.

The city grows upward

The improved economic conditions in Europe during the 11th century encouraged people to migrate from the countryside to the towns. The best possible use was made of the space inside the walls and, in Italy, this led to the "tower-houses," buildings that were sometimes 200–230 feet (60–70 meters) tall. They served as dwelling-places but also as refuges and fortresses during periods of strife with rival families. Few remain today because the defeat of a family usually led to the demolition, or at least the lowering, of its tower.

Above: A view of the walls and towers of Florence, Italy, in the mid-14th century.

Below: The busy port of Lübeck, along with nearby Hamburg, was a founder of the Hanseatic League of merchant cities.

Buildings in Northern Europe

Stone was less commonly used in Northern Europe and most private dwellings were build of wood. This seriously increased the risk of fires because, apart from domestic hearths, each town also included bakers' ovens and the forges of blacksmiths and other metalworkers.

Serfdom

Until the 13th century, those who worked the land were either free peasants, to whom the local nobility had ceded some land, or serfs who labored on their properties. The serfs were tied to the land they worked and when it was sold or ceded, they also were passed on to the next owner. Peasants and serfs owed labor to their lords, work they were obliged to carry out without payment, that might involve repairs to the castle, building roads and bridges, or setting up a new mill.

Fresco in the Castle of Buonconsiglio, Trent, Italy

Many churches and castles were decorated with scenes from daily life. This fresco, in the Eagle's Tower in Buonconsiglio Castle, comes from a cycle showing work carried out in each month of the year. It shows the months of July (1) and August (2). In July, peasants are cutting grass with scythes (3), and forking and raking it to dry (4). There are men fishing on a lake (5), and a man with a falcon (6) about to go hunting. In the foreground, a nobleman presents a game bird to a lady (7). In August, the peasants are harvesting gain (8), carrying it in on carts (9), and forking it into a barn for the winter (10). In the foreground, a group of nobles stand in a walled garden holding hunting falcons (11). One man is plucking a piece of fruit from a vine (12).

Ordinary farmers did not own a plow (below), which was used for cutting furrows in the soil and turning it over before sowing seed. Plows usually belonged to the local lord, or were jointly owned by all the people of a village.

A highly prized tree

Woodlands were of vital importance to the medieval rural economy. They were places for hunting, raising pigs, or gathering fruits, berries, mushrooms, and roots. Wood was cut and used both for fuel and as a building material. One of the most highly prized trees was the chestnut, which produced edible nuts and hard-wearing wood that was used for making beams and casks, as well as many farming implements.

The Countryside

The countryside underwent many changes over the centuries. The great forests of the early Middle Ages, broken by a few laboriously worked cultivated areas, gradually gave way to the well-ordered fields of the late medieval era, when different crops were grown in the same field, according to carefully conceived plans. A vine could be made to grow up against a fruit tree, and grains like wheat and barley could be grown between the rows of vines. Peasant families were usually large, and sons continued to live under their father's roof after they were married to make it easier to work the larger farms.

These illustrations from around 1300 show some of the goods that peasants had to pay to the lord of the manor.

Above: There was a blacksmith in every village. He had many important jobs, such as shoeing horses, and making and repairing farm and household implements, including hoes, rakes, plow blades, knifes, pots, and pans.

The village

Between the 9th and 12th centuries, a new kind of settlement appeared: the village. Before this, the peasants lived scattered in the countryside, cultivating their plots for land. With the birth of the village, which was generally fortified, the surrounding land was divided into three bands (the vegetable gardens nearest the walls, then the vines, and finally, fields of grain), and the peasants all lived together in the castle-village, where the harvest and farm implements were stored and animals housed.

Beekeeping

Bees were extremely important during the Middle Ages. Their wax was used to make candles, essential for lighting homes and churches. Their honey was used as a sweetener (cane sugar was only known in the Islamic world), and it was also used in the preparation of many medicines.

The grape harvest

The vine was widely cultivated, and wine was the main drink in many parts of Europe. Each piece of farmland was usually flanked by rows of vines, raised from the ground and supported by stakes or trees. In some areas in the Mediterranean, vines were grown at ground level without supports.

The mill

The water mill, first introduced by the Romans, became widely adopted during the 11th century. Although it was chiefly used to grind cereals, it also served other purposes, such as driving the pump to irrigate the fields, the bellows at the forge, or the blades for milling cloth (to make it softer and stronger). Mills were under the management of the local landowners, who rented them to the peasants. A kind of mill that used wind instead of water as a source of energy was brought to Europe from the Arab world during the 11th century.

Florentine gold florin
From the time of Charlemagne the leading currency in Europe had been made of silver. In 1252, the first gold coin was struck in Florence, the florin (so called because one side bore a lily, the emblem of Florence). It became immediately popular in Europe and several mints began to copy it.

Two of the "safer" currencies of the 13th century: a Florentine florin and a genovina, a Genoese gold coin. They were struck and guaranteed by the mints in Florence and Genoa and accepted in all Eastern and Western markets.

Merchants and Trade

D uring the invasions and migrations there was a decrease in production and commerce, but in the 11th century there was an economic recovery all over Europe. Markets and fairs were held in many towns (famous ones included those in Champagne, in France), and attracted traders and buyers from near and far. Many of these markets coincided with religious festivals and, indeed, merchants congregated in places where they would find groups of pilgrims who were anxious to buy. Arab and Byzantine activity meant this was also a time of increased exchange with Eastern countries. The increase in trade also led to the creation of guilds for merchants and, later, for craftsmen. Guilds were organizations formed to protect the interests of specific groups. New coins began to circulate in Europe.

The Bishop's Fair, Sens, France
Markets were held in many towns and villages throughout the Middle Ages. People came from the surrounding countryside to buy and sell food, clothes, tools, and whatever they could not make at home. In the early centuries much of the trade was barter – the exchanging of different kinds of goods without paying money. This image from a 14th-century French manuscript shows a market that was held for two weeks every June on the Plains of St. Denis. It shows sheep (1) being brought for sale while merchants sit in their tent-like booths (2) offering their various wares. The tent on the right (3) shows wine and beer being served to thirsty merchants. In the center, the bishop (4) presides over all the goings-on.

Right: These European merchants are shown arriving at a port in the Persian Gulf on their return journey from the East. They have a camel and an elephant on board. Animals were often brought back to Europe and were usually given to princes or wealthy nobles.

Spices from the East

Spices were the main import from the East. Merchants dealt in all the most popular ones like pepper, ginger, and cinnamon. Pepper came from India and Marco Polo, the Venetian merchant who traveled much in the East, wrote that he had seen enormous plantations of pepper in Malaysia. The Arab merchants carried goods from these distant lands to Mediterranean countries.

The Hanseatic League

In the 13th century, trading cities along the North Sea and Baltic coasts started to band together to protect their common interests. The port of Hamburg was an important member of this Hanseatic League, or Hansa (which comes from an Old German word meaning "company"). By the mid-1300s, the League included all the larger German cities, and by 1400 it had members in 160 towns in Northern Europe. Meetings were held at Lübeck, where members discussed how to help each other gain control of foreign trade and fight pirates and bandits. If a town refused to join the League, the merchants of that town found it impossible to sell their goods in profitable markets. The League gained control of the fur trade with Russia, the fish trade with Norway and Sweden, and the wool trade with Belgium. Members also developed a system of commercial laws, to protect themselves against others. The Hansa lasted as a powerful force until 1669.

Below: These signs are the trademarks of members of the guild of clothmakers in Florence. Trade was closely organized and monitored. Guilds controlled markets, weights and measures, and, to some extent, prices.

Guilds

Merchants and tradesmen got together to form guilds. The main purpose of these groups was to protect trade. They were often religious in character, and took part in charity work as well as protecting their members. They became an important influence in town life and government. Some presented the religious mystery plays that were the main form of medieval theater. They enforced high standards of production, but they disliked competition and resisted new members and methods.

Money-changers

The first money-changers appeared in town markets during the 13th century. They changed money and took deposits, but if they failed to fulfill their undertakings, their stalls were "broken" by the town guards (giving rise to the expression "bankrupt," from *bank* and the Latin word *ruptus*, which means *broken*). Later, as trade flourished, specialized banks were created with representatives in the major towns and cities.

The city of Hamburg grew up around the Hammaburg castle in about 825. Standing between the Alster and Elbe Rivers, it was a good natural port. A founding member of the Hanseatic League, Hamburg was an important center of trade throughout the Middle Ages.

Medieval towns had no street lights. The townspeople often employed watchmen to patrol the town at night – these men carried a lantern like this one, and perhaps a cudgel as well.

Candles

Aside from oil lamps, candles were the only source of artificial light. They were made by pouring molten wax, or animal fat, into molds which contained a length of wick. When they had solidified, they were scraped to remove imperfections and sold in the grocer's shop, where sponges, spices, and medicinal herbs could also be bought.

Goods were weighed on pan scales, or steelyard scales, shown here hanging on the wall. These are both instruments of Roman origin and remained in use for centuries.

The cloth merchant

Florence was at the heart of the cloth trade. Besides the usual locally produced cloths in wool and cotton, there was also a trade in precious, decorated, and embroidered fabrics. Silk produced in Italy and Spain was exported all over Europe and came into common use in the 14th century. For the wealthier classes, there was a specialized production of fine and fancy cloths like brocades, satins, and velvets.

Teaching, Culture, and Science

The Middle Ages have often been considered an unexciting time from an artistic and scientific point of view. Today, however, we know that important changes took place during this period which laid the basis for many aspects of contemporary culture. In the literary field, a vital contribution was made by the copyists who handed down poetic and scientific works, frequently through Arab sources. Emperors and popes fully understood the importance of culture, and in the 13th century, they were the benefactors of many new universities. Progress was also made in the fields of science and technology, especially in the later Middle Ages when urban growth provided a stimulus for carrying out major town planning projects.

This illustration shows a doctor setting a broken leg in a cast apparently made of straw or wood.

During the 14th century, a terrible disease, known as the plague or Black Death, spread across Europe, killing about one-third of the people. This doctor's costume shows that the danger of infection was understood, though no one knew how it happened. The "beak" contained strong-smelling herbs, which he hoped would "clean" the air that he breathed.

Medieval healers used herbs to treat their patients. The two herbs shown here, wormwood (left) and lungwort (right) were used, respectively, against fleas and chest disorders.

Medicine
There were two kinds of doctors: the physician, whose work was limited to taking the pulse and examining urine, and who cured the sick with the aid of medicines made from herbs; and the surgeon, who needed a good grasp of anatomy. The surgeon carried out external operations like lancing or amputation, almost always performed without an anaesthetic.

Mechanical clocks
The first mechanical clocks appeared in Europe at the end of the 13th century, gradually taking the place of bell-ringing. They had counterweight mechanisms and struck the hours. These were public clocks and were set on high towers so they could be seen and heard from all over the city, signaling important times of day such as the opening and closing of the city-gates, changing of the guard, and the call to public meetings.

Cardinal Ugo of Provence, France shown in 1352 wearing a pair of glasses.

Clip-on spectacles, of immense help to copyists and illuminators.

Spectacles
The very first spectacles were made in Pisa toward the end of the 13th century, but the center of production soon became Venice, where glasswork was an ancient skill. The lenses were made by grinding the glass against a cup-shaped tool coated with sand, and then cleaning and polishing it with very fine powder.

Map making
In this geographical chart showing the known world in the 13th century, the holy city of Jerusalem is set in the center. Journeys and expeditions by land and sea supplied information for the production of increasingly accurate maps.

The copyists

We owe our knowledge of early literature to the monks who were engaged as copyists, or scribes. Apart from copying contemporary texts, they also had the task of transcribing early texts by hand, long before the invention of printing. Copyists used a sloping bench, and their instruments included a pen or calamus (a sharpened reed); a scraper for removing errors; a ruler; and callipers, for tracing the lines for writing.

Illuminated manuscripts

The pages of manuscripts were often embellished with illuminations, real works of art, in which the initial letter of a text was decorated with religious subjects, scenes from daily life, or abstract designs, often containing an allusion to the text itself. A book involved the work of a copyist, an illuminator, and a binder.

Students attending a lesson

Universities in Europe developed out of cathedral and monastery schools. During the 12th century, these schools were still under the authority of the Church and their chief aim was to produce high-ranking clergy. By the 13th century, many early universities had their own statutes, according to which students and teachers decided on subjects and methods of teaching. Over the course of time, universities developed specializations: Paris was renowned for Theology, Bologna for Law, and Padua for Medicine.

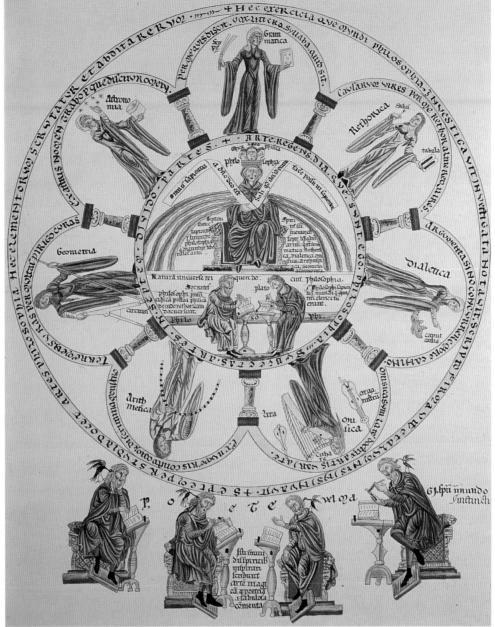

Philosophy and the Seven Liberal Arts
This 12th-century German miniature shows the subjects that were taught at medieval universities. The outer circle represents philosophy (1), an all-encompassing discipline. The liberal arts were divided into seven areas: grammar (2), rhetoric (3), dialectic, or logical disputation (4), music (5), arithmetic (6), geometry (7), and astronomy (8). The figures below represent the four literary disciplines (9).

Art and Architecture

From the 10th to the 13th centuries, the leading artistic field was architecture, particularly church architecture. It took the form of solid stone buildings, worthy of being called the "fortresses of God." This style was later called Romanesque, because it combined traces of ancient Roman art with the spirit of Christianity and the energy of the Germanic peoples who had settled in Western Europe. This was followed by the Gothic style, whose name was originally intended in a derogatory manner, because it was thought to have destroyed the classical tradition. In fact, the light and slender forms typical of Gothic architecture paved the way for renewed energy that soon appeared in all the arts, from architecture, sculpture, painting and illumination, to goldsmithery, furnishings, and tapestries. Medieval knowledge also underwent a revival in the 12th century with "scholasticism," a term that encompassed the whole range of intellectual endeavor in the Middle Ages (philosophy, theology, and science). At the same time, the spoken language (the vernacular) acquired new dignity in literature and music, as is shown by the poems of the troubadours.

Many Romanesque churches were decorated with beautiful statues, like this one which shows Pythagoras, from the cathedral at Chartres, in France.

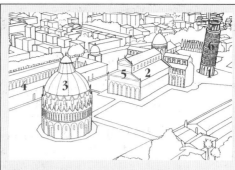

The Cathedral, Baptistry, and Tower at Pisa, Italy

From the 11th to the 13th centuries, the town of Pisa on the west coast of Italy was a rich and powerful trading city. It was at that time that the Pisans built the the monuments in the Campo dei Miracoli (Field of Miracles). These include the world-famous leaning tower (1), the cathedral (2), the baptistry (3), and the Campo Santo cemetery (4). The cathedral is one of the most impressive and majestic of all the Romanesque churches. It has an ornately decorated façade (5), the motif of which is repeated in the arcaded galleries running around the tower behind it (6). The baptistry was partly remodeled in Gothic style at a later date. The composition is one of the most beautiful in the history of architecture and dramatically expressed the new age of building that characterized the time.

A gargoyle, or water spout, from the Cathedral of Notre Dame, in Paris, France. Gargoyles were commonly used on Gothic buildings.

Below: The gatehouse of the monastery of Lorsch, near Worms, in Germany. The monastery was founded in the 8th century, and the entrance is based on the triumphal arches of the classical world. Local architects tried to copy early Christian churches, but they also added many typically German features.

This stained glass window from Chartres Cathedral shows the parable of the Good Samaritan. It is designed to be read from top to bottom and from left to right.

Stained glass windows

Stained glass windows, whose radiant light beautifies the interiors of the major cathedrals in Europe, were first produced in medieval times. Like the cycles of fresco paintings in medieval churches, they illustrate scenes from the Bible, helping the vast majority of worshipers (who did not know how to read) to become familiar with the Bible. The design for a stained glass window was first drawn on a wooden board. Glass cutters then laid pieces of colored glass over this and cut them to the required shapes with a red-hot iron point. The details were painted later in enamel colors and sealed by firing.

Byzantine architecture had a range of traditions and styles of its own. Most Byzantine churches had domed roofs, like this small church built in Calabria, in southern Italy, during the 10th century.

Below: The little church of San Juan de Baños de Cerrato is the finest surviving example of Visigoth architecture in Spain. It dates back to 661.

A richly decorated Romanesque door from the church at Kilpeck, England, dating from around 1140.

The cathedral at Burgos, in Spain, was founded in 1221. The tall Gothic towers were added in the 15th century.

This ornate 12th century carving comes from the doorway of a church in Arles, France. It shows Christ surrounded by the symbols for Matthew, Mark, Luke, and John.

Regional variety

The main trend in medieval architecture was the move from the sturdy early buildings of the Germanic invaders (see opposite), through the strong but graceful Romanesque (see photo of the complex at Pisa, above), and on to the almost impossibly slender spires of the Gothic revolution (see left). Yet each of these styles was treated differently according to which part of Europe it was built in. Local ideas and traditions mingled with the new ideas, giving each building a distinctive regional character.

The Lady and the Unicorn

This tapestry is one of a cycle of six now kept in the Cluny Museum of the Middle Ages, in Paris. Each of the first five tapestries represents one of the five senses – sight, hearing, taste, touch, and smell – while the sixth symbolizes the renunciation of the senses. They all show the lady (1) and her maid (2) with a lion (3) and a unicorn (4). In this scene, the lady is carefully replacing a necklace into a casket (5) held out to her by her maidservant. A bright blue tent (6) opening behind the lady draws our attention to her. The inscription on the tent (7), in French, *A mon seul désir*, can be translated "in accordance with my will," and means that the lady is freely renouncing the passions of the senses. The bright red background is covered with tiny flowers (8) and four different kinds of flowering trees (9). The many animals shown include rabbits (10), a goat (11), three dogs (12), a monkey (13), a lamb (14), and two kinds of birds (15). Historians are unsure exactly where the tapestries were woven and who the artist was, but they all agree that these are among the most beautiful tapestries created at this time.

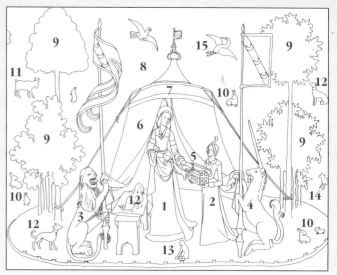

Icons

Icons are works of art in the Eastern Orthodox Christian tradition showing sacred people or events. These religious pictures, developed originally in Byzantine art, were the subject of a dispute over the use of religious images (called the Iconoclastic Controversy – see page 13) in the 8th and 9th centuries.

Above: This detail from an icon shows the first two Russian saints, Boris and Gleb, who became Christians in 988.

The painted cross

During the Middle Ages, the painted cross, derived from Byzantine art, became a favorite subject. It illustrated the Crucifixion of Christ and was often suspended from the triumphal arch or set between the part of the church reserved for clerics and the central nave. Christ was originally depicted as still alive, his eyes open and his body firm, unmarked by suffering or death. But in the 13th century, this was superseded by the image of the "suffering" Christ, shown at the moment of death, with drooping head and limp heavy body hanging lifeless from the cross. This crucifixion is based on a work by the Italian painter, Cimabue.

The Celtic cross

Celtic art, famous for its illuminated sacred texts, also produced stone crosses carved in relief with Biblical scenes. They date from the 9th and 10th centuries when monastic life was fully established in Ireland.

Woodcarving

Wood was an essential material for building houses, churches, bridges, and many other constructions throughout the Middle Ages. It was also a popular material for carvings, and one of the most common subjects in Romanesque wood carving was the Virgin Mary seated with the child Jesus in her lap. When the carving was complete it was painted in bright colors.

During the 12th century, the cult of the Virgin Mary grew in Western Europe. This early 13th century statue in carved and painted wood, comes from Cataluny, in Spain.

Right: Detail from a richly decorated altar in St. Ambrogio, Milan, Italy.

Jewelry and metalworking

Medieval jewelers and metalworkers produced some extremely fine work, including clasps, pins, belt buckles, pendants, necklaces, and crowns. Craftsmen mastered all the skilled techniques, such as embossing, filigree, granulation, and open-work, but they were particularly fond of inlay, and ornamented their pieces by setting them with precious stones or glass paste.

Most art during the Middle Ages had a religious theme or was commissioned by members of the Church. The crosier (above), or head of a bishop's staff, was carved in ivory during the 11th century. Left, a reliquary, a special container to hold a saint's sacred remains or objects.

Scholasticism

Scholasticism was the name given to theological and philosophical thought when, from the 11th century, most knowledge was imparted by the religious schools attached to monasteries or cathedrals. These were later joined by the universities, which were free associations of teachers and pupils. Scholasticism's aim was to establish a harmony between human reason and belief in the sacred revelation as expressed in the Bible. While distinct from each other, faith and reason were united in the search for one and the same truth. The leading exponent of scholasticism was St. Thomas Aquinas (1226-1274), who taught in Paris, Bologna, and Naples.

Daily Life

History used to be about wars, kings, queens, and the life and times of important people. But during the 20th century, many historians began to study how people went about their daily lives. They believed that knowing what people ate, how they dressed, slept, and amused themselves was of fundamental importance in understanding the past. Modern historians still study rich and powerful people, and large-scale events like wars or economic recessions, but they also focus on the everyday lives of ordinary people. During the Middle Ages, the vast majority of people were poor and lived in the countryside. Wealthy people lived in country manors or comfortable city houses, and enjoyed a variety of sports, games, and entertainments.

Wealthy people enjoyed sumptuous banquets. Forks had not been introduced to Europe at this time, and people used knives and their hands to eat.

Bathing

Public baths existed in the Middle Ages, run either by private citizens or by the town authorities. Hot or cold baths were available, but they were also places to meet people, eat, drink, or find entertainment. The baths themselves were great wooden vats lined with a sheet, often covered with a canopy or curtain to keep in the warmth and steam.

Children in medieval times

Many children had hard lives in the Middle Ages. Newborn babies were frequently abandoned, and many hospitals were set up to take in foundlings. These institutions assumed parental responsibility and care, although the children could be reclaimed at any time. Even the children of rich families were sometimes handed over to monasteries or other families so that inheritances did not have to be divided among too many heirs.

A magistrate decides the fate of two orphans, illustration from a 14th century codex.

Serfs and peasants lived in basic conditions. They often shared their simple homes with their animals.

Food and cooking

Medieval cooking was influenced by Arab and Eastern cuisines, and used a large number of spices, many of which came from the Middle East: saffron, ginger, cinnamon, and many more. People who could not afford the luxury of spices used garlic, onions, and fragrant herbs. The tables of the rich and the nobility were laden with meat, served with various kinds of sauce, from the peppery to the bitter-sweet, while the humbler citizens dined chiefly on grain soups. The most common drink, in all walks of life, was wine.

Dress: a question of status

These young people playing blind-man's-buff, a game known all over Europe, belong to the rich merchant class or the nobility. We see this from their stylish clothes made of richly colored fabrics like velvet, wool, and silk, of Flemish or Italian manufacture. The peasants and the hired workers wore much simpler clothes made from poorer materials (cotton, linen, or cheap wool) produced by less skilled local workers. A really heavy, warm garment was so expensive that it could be purchased only a few times in the course of a lifetime.

Housing for rich and poor

The homes of the poorer people were little more than humble shelters for sleeping, eating, and storing the bare necessities of life. The furniture would at most have included a large bed where the whole family slept together, a trunk for storing bed linen and clothing, a table, and a cupboard for cereals and a few kitchen utensils. The houses of the nobility were on quite another scale, well-arranged and decorated with frescoes. Although pieces of furniture were finer and more numerous, they were the same as those in the homes of the poor. At most, there might also have been a large chest for storing valuable objects, perhaps those brought by the wife as her dowry, or the deeds of a property.

Children Playing, Pieter Bruegel

This picture was painted by the Flemish painter Bruegel in 1560. In this view of a town, the streets are full of children playing. There are more than 250 children, wrestling (1), climbing (2), swinging (3), playing with barrels (4), knucklebones (5), and masks (6). In the foreground, children are bowling wooden hoops with sticks (7). Further back, there are children playing leapfrog (8) and doing headstands (9).

Musician playing a lute, and a sheet of music made around 1420.

Music and musicians

Music was very popular, and even great lords and kings knew how to play. Entertainers, called troubadours, composed words and music. They moved from court to court, followed by minstrels, whose task it was to play and sing. The most common instruments were the harp and the lute.

Hunting

One of the nobility's favorite pastimes was hunting, which called for dogs, horses, weapons, and beaters. Boar and deer were the most sought-after prey, and poachers faced the death penalty. Emperor Frederick II hunted with falcons, a practice that was introduced to Europe by Eastern nomadic peoples, and he wrote a treatise on the subject which became famous.

Jousting

Jousting was a form of combat between two knights that took place before the lords and ladies of the court. First recorded in France in the early 12th century, most jousting competitions were held in Northern Europe. In the early days, extremely violent bouts took place between two teams of knights but later, blunted weapons were adopted, reducing the number of victims. Real jousting, one-to-one fighting, was also regulated, and wooden fences were built to separate the combatants and prevent head-on collisions.

The Birth of Nations

Rising prosperity, a growing middle class, and an artistic and cultural revival fueled the need for a new type of society, which would be stable and efficient and could guarantee peace to its citizens. This led to the creation of nation-states, united under kings who were entrusted with the task of governing "for the common good." By the late 13th century, nation-states in Europe were already organized in a modern manner: they had armies for defense; fiscal systems to collect the money to pay for the government; bureaucrats to implement the kings' wishes; and judges to punish those who broke the laws. The voice of the people also began to find a hearing through assemblies that were set up to support and control the king. In England, Parliament came into being; while in Spain, the *Cortes* were established; and in France, the *Estates General* set up.

The English monarchy

William the Conqueror (above) became the first Norman king of England in 1066. The authority of the crown was reinforced by Henry II Plantagenet (1154–1189), who severely restricted the rights of the barons. His marriage to Eleanor of Aquitaine brought with it great wealth and extensive territories in France, but also led to the Hundred Years' War. When the English lost, a bloody civil war broke out in England. It was called the War of the Roses, because of the emblems of the two contending houses of York (the white rose) and Lancaster (the red). Henry VII Tudor, a distant relation of the House of Lancaster, emerged victorious. Under him and his descendants, safe on their island, England played little part in political events on the European continent.

During the Hundred Years' War between England and France, Joan of Arc (c.1412–31) claimed to hear the voices of saints urging her to lead the French army against the English. The French won at Orléans, opening the way to French unity and victory over the English.

This vase dates from the time of the Nasrid dynasty in Granada, the last of the Muslim dynasties in Spain.

Regaining Spain

On the Iberian peninsula, Spain began to emerge as Muslim domination was gradually overcome. Reconstruction was made more difficult by the rivalry between the Christian princes. In 1469 the heir to the throne of the kingdom of Aragon married Isabella of Castile and this marriage united the two most powerful families in the land. After the defeat of Muslim rule in Granada in 1492 Spain became a single nation-state.

The making of France

The kingdom of France was formed around the lands of the French dukes, owners of the Parisian region. The founder of the ruling dynasty was Hugh Capet, crowned in 987. Over the centuries, his descendants gradually extended their rule over the surrounding area, making subjects of the local lords who aspired to independence. Philip the Fair (1285–1314) clashed with the pope with the support of the Estates General, made up of nobles, clerics, and members of the bourgeoisie, finally demonstrating that he alone was in command in France. The unifying effort of the Capet family gave birth to France, which remained united despite the claims of the English crown.

The Magna Carta

The popularity of the English monarchy reached its lowest point with King John (1199–1216), who was responsible for the loss of many of England's territories in France. Taking advantage of his weakness, the barons forced him to sign the Magna Carta Libertatum which, by according various privileges to nobles, clerics, and the wealthy bourgeoisie, set limitations on his own power. Moreover, the Magna Carta established that no free man could be arrested and condemned without a proper trial by law before a tribunal composed of his peers. This document is considered a great step in human history because, for the first time, the relationship between sovereign and subject was regulated and set out in writing.

Scandinavia and Eastern Europe

Despite many difficulties, the kingdoms of Denmark, Sweden, and Norway were also established during the 13th century and, in 1320, the kingdom of Poland was founded. The Russian monarchy sprang from among the rich and powerful Grand Dukes of Moscow and during the 14th century, Ivan III (1440–1505) adopted the title of czar. While Germany remained a divided country, a new great power began to emerge in the very heart of Europe under the control of an Austrian family, the Habsburgs. By 1382, they had extended their rule as far as the Adriatic, and conquered the port of Trieste. In 1437, Albert II took the title of emperor and after this date, the emperor of the German Holy Roman Empire was always a Habsburg. Acquisition of this grand title helped the Habsburgs to advance themselves by making politically advantageous marriages.

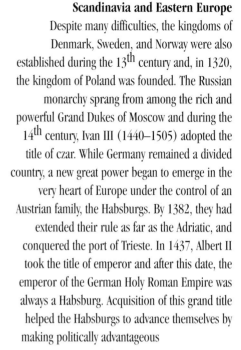

The first king of Poland, Boleslaw the Brave (reigned 1024–1025), who reorganized the Church in Poland, making it responsible directly to the pope.

─ HOLY ROMAN EMPIRE	UNION OF KALMAR
■ HABSBURG TERRITORIES	UNION OF KREVO
LUXEMBOURG TERRITORIES	■ OTTOMAN EMPIRE

■ CROWN OF ARAGON
BURGUNDIAN TERRITORIES
ANGEVIN TERRITORIES

The Model Parliament

The English word parliament comes from "parly," which were talks that the king had with groups of advisors. In 1295, the English king, Edward I, called the largest assembly ever, to raise money to wage war against Philip of France. This became known as the Model Parliament. As shown here in this 16th-century illustration, it included King Edward (1), his vassals, King Alexander III of Scotland (2) and Prince Llywelyn ap Gruffydd of Wales (3), along with the Archbishops of Canterbury (4) and York (5). The others are the Lords Spiritual (6) to his right, and the Lords Temporal to his left (7), and the judges of the realm sitting on woolsacks in between (8).

Political map of Europe c. 1400.

Index

The publishers would like to thank the following picture libraries and photographers for permission to reproduce their photos:

Cover: *Guidoriccio da Fogliano all'assedio di Monte Massi*, Siena, Palazzo Pubblico (Scala Group, Florence)
7 Scala Group, Florence; 9 Scala Group, Florence; 10 Scala Group, Florence; 12-13 Scala Group, Florence; 15 The Art Archive / Dagli Orti (A), London; 17 Scala Group, Florence; 18-19 Scala Group, Florence; 21 Scala Group, Florence; 22 Scala Group, Florence; 24 Archivi Alinari, Florence; 27 Claus Hansmann, München; 28-29 Archivi Alinari, Florence; 30 Scala Group, Florence; 33 Archivi Alinari, Florence.